Politically INCORRECT Lexicon

by Dr Peter Mullen

First Published 2012

Bretwalda Books
Unit 8, Fir Tree Close, Epsom, Surrey KT17 3LD
www.BretwaldaBooks.com

To receive an e-catalogue of our complete range of books send an email to info@BretwaldaBooks.com

ISBN 978-1-907791-42-0

Bretwalda Books Ltd

Foreword
By Quentin Letts

Peter Mullen is that rare thing, a fiery, right-wing, 21st century Anglican priest. At the mention of his name, certain dignitaries of the London diocese fan their hands and have to be laid flat on a pew until the moment has passed. Father Mullen gives stalwarts of the "Church Times" and the "Tablet" an

attack of the vapours, popping the tops of the stovepipe hats those modern puritans wear. This short, bustling, slightly lop-sided Yorkshireman, succinct and scintillating in the pulpit, is a generous, forthright priest. He has long been unbending in his assaults on the Church's gormless modernisations. He is vigorous and funny, indignant at the disintegrating culture whose supposed guardians - today's Sanhedrin - have been accomplices to neglect and decline. Mullen rejoices in the majesty of the Book of Common Prayer and, rightly, considers newer liturgy a cheap pretender.

We live in a time of spiritual humming and hawing. This is the age of ethical prevarication. Society hungers for certitude but instead man clerics offer a form of multiple-choice morality, couched in cotton-wool words. Oh, the fakeness of so much modern language. The politically correct jargon spouted by the indulging Left is designed to smudge issues, to avoid the truth. That is why this little snorter of a book is so welcome. It strips away deceit. Opacity rhymes with mendacity.

Jesus urged us to speak our minds. Peter Mullen does just that. He grabs us by the windpipe and forces us to see the truth behind dishonest phrases - "lies", as we used to call them. In the past half-century the Church of England has mumbled its message. Such a charge could never be levelled at Mullen and we should thank God for his peppery pugnacity.

Tragedy

Any accident, train crash, mass murder or earthquake etc. Especially a terrorist atrocity. Or a British tennis player failing to win Wimbledon *Formerly,* the fall from greatness because of a deep character flaw. E.g. Hamlet is foiled by his indecision and Caesar by ambition etc. See **atrocity, outrage.**

Good (l)

Meaningless. *Good* is anything anyone says it is; what feels good to you.

Good (2)

As in *I'm good* the standard ignoramus replacement for *I'm well, thank you*

Terminally ill

Dying

Learning difficulties

The most recent development in the euphemising series: *Backward, slow, mentally-subnormal, mentally deficient, intellectually impaired* etc. Someone lolling about, barely able to speak or co-ordinate his bodily movements etc is said to have *learning difficulties*

Underprivileged

Spurious. A solecism. cf *overprivileged, privileged* etc. But where everyone is described as to some degree *privileged* the word loses all meaning

Liberal

ironic As in *liberal establishment* (i.e. the BBC) or *liberal Christians*. i.e. those who persecute anyone who does not share their views. Liberals believe themselves to be broad-minded. For *liberal* read *totalitarian*

Tolerance

Formerly a desirable quality, as in one who *tolerates* those of whom he disapproves. But see **live and let live**. Currently an undesirable quality, its possession suggesting that there is such a thing as normal human behaviour

Refute

To gainsay, deny, shout down etc. *formerly* a series of arguments disproving a proposition

Music (1)

obsolete The serious orchestral and choral music of the western tradition from about the year 1500.

Music (2)

Currently noise. Especially public noises reviewed in **quality newspapers.** *e.g The F***ing Decibels provided a night to remember with their gig at the Albert Hall*

Judgemental (1)

Obsolete The capacity to make judgements, one of the highest qualities in human beings.

Judgemental (2)

Currently The offensive practice of claiming that some things are good and others less good. See also **Elitist**

Elitist

Perjorative. Asserting that things/activities differ in value e.g. *Beethoven is better than The F***ing Decibels* . Strangely it is not elitist to claim that, for instance, Chelsea FC are better than Hartlepool United or that one brand of **mobile phone** is superior to another.

Discrimination

Archaic Refined and developed tastefulness, the ability to recognise quality, able to tell one thing from another – as in *he knows his onions*. Now only *pejorative. except* between brews of beer, types of **trainers**, **mobile phones** etc See **Elitist** and **Judgmental**

Indoctrination

That which the church used to do legitimately, now done by the government. See **Global warming. Antiracism** etc

Peacekeeping

…as in *United Nations peacekeeping force*. A company of soldiers that stands by and observes massacre and genocide – in e.g. Bosnia, Sudan etc

Closure

As in *Now the man who murdered our teenage daughter has been sentenced to life imprisonment, we have achieved closure*. i.e. all the moral and emotional consequences of the crime can now be forgotten. See **Move on**

Move on

What people are said to be able to do when they have achieved **closure.** *Also*, what politicians want to do when caught wasting public money on pet projects, breaking election promises, telling lies etc.

Democracy (1)

Formerly an open system of government which, while implementing the wishes of the majority, respected the rights of minorities.

Democracy (2)

Currently Counting heads and enforcing the majority view while denying the wishes of minorities, for instance, foxhunting and smoking. However, in cases where the majority support an issue disapproved of by the **liberal establishment** – **capital punishment**, strict immigration control, disallowing blasphemy etc – the views of the majority are always overruled

The grieving process

Psychobabble for the five stages of grief that bereaved persons are said endure in sequence – whether they know it or not. See **Dogma**

Dogma (1)

arch What **primitive** people used to believe – e.g. the Christian Creed, the Ten Commandments etc. Belief in or the enforcement of such dogma is a bad thing.

Dogma (2)
The latest fashions in scientific thought. e.g. the big bang, global warming etc. Belief in such dogma is a good thing.

Dogma (3)
Any injunction validated by the alleged findings of modern science. e.g *Salt/red meat/cheese are bad for you.* Enforcement of such dogma is a good thing

Gender (I)
Obsolete used of nouns in the days when it was thought there was a subject called *grammar.* See **Primitive**

Gender (2)
Currently Sex

Light entertainment (I)
An oxymoron – as in *young people;* **reality television**; *French Resistance;* **popular music** and *radio comedy.*

Light entertainment (2)
Heavy tedium

Adult (I)
Childish.

Adult (2)
Filthy, pornographic

Primitive
Old. e.g. classical Greek philosophy, Moses, St Paul, the Christian religion. Anything predating the iphone

Sex-education

Enlightened inculcation of promiscuity among children by telling them how easy it is to procure an abortion. See **birth control**

Birth control

Abortion

The Peace

The noisiest part of modern church services in which unsuspecting visitors are shaken by the hand, kissed, cuddled, hugged or otherwise molested and grinned at as an expression of **Christian fellowship**

Christian fellowship

A congregation of mawkish literalists, arms raised, repeating tirelessly in chorus words that weren't worth singing once

Partner

Any shack-up sexual relationship that lasts longer than three days

Marriage

An ornament. Any coupling between two people of whatever sex that is intended to last longer than a one-night stand

Feelings

The licence for the public expression of any emotion. Journalistic cliché. The authenticating criteria of the **sentimental society**, as in *How did you feel when your mother/sister/hamster died?* Also *I can't help the way I feel.*

Sentimental society

Public life. The people. e.g. the people's Princess/**the People's** Olympics. A development *especially* since the death of the Princess in 1997 and the subsequent **Dianafication** of society. See also **feelings**

Reforms

Destruction. As in *NHS reforms* or *educational reforms*

University (1)

Formerly a centre of educational excellence where older folk passed on years of accumulated learning and wisdom to younger folk

University (2)

Government-funded establishments which outlaw **discrimination, judgementalism, elitism** and the concept of excellence. Former technical colleges turned into playschools. Places with classes such as *golf with catering* and *cosmetic studies.*

University (3)

Training school for careers in consumerism e.g *golf studies with ten pin bowling; travel, tourism & hairdressing*

Standards

Those things which decline

Martyr (Islam)

Mass murderer, suicide bomber. Someone who takes the lives of others for his faith

Martyr (Christian)

Someone who gives his own life for his faith

Rights (I)

Social and legal attributes which are regarded as universal – But see **liberal establishment** which exempts the Muslim states from this requirement.

Rights (2)

Government guarantees through the process of legal fictions to exculpate felons from the consequences of their crimes – e.g. the refusal to prosecute the hijacking of a civilian aircraft by illegal immigrants or the refusal to repatriate a foreign murderer because to do so *would deny him the right to a family life*

Rights (3)

Legal innovations by which a householder may not erect a barbed wire barrier across his roof in case this causes injury to burglars

Critical but stable

Said of accident victims. Contradiction in terms. Something that is in the moment of being judged, in the balance – precisely unstable

Wicked

archaic indescribably evil. Currently the ultimate accolade among all things *cool*

Accessible

So stupid and dumbed down that even readers of **tabloid newspapers** can understand what's going on

Brings alive

Spoils, ruins. As in *brings Shakespeare alive.* i.e. cutting the dialogue, cutting out politically-incorrect language, dressing the cast of (say) *Julius Caesar* as Nazis and transferring the action from late Republican Rome to 1930s Berlin.

Love

archaic that which desires the good of the beloved. Currently, sex, Schmaltz, sentimentality, mawkishness, funny feeling in the tummy etc.

Concert

Noise, nuisance, disturbance, breach of the peace, occasion for public drug-taking, casual fornication etc

Peace process

An extended programme of sucking up to terrorists and giving in to their demands

Uses

Abuses: as of illegal drugs

Youths

Young people when they are misbehaving

Young people

Youths who undertake charitable works

Choice

A key word in advertising and political propaganda used to promote the illusion that there are qualitative differences between washing machines/DVDs/pre-cooked meals/state schools/NHS hospitals etc

God (I)

obsolete For the mass of the population, an expletive; a swear-word

God (2)

For the bishops, a metaphor for left wing political ideals. (see also **Allah**)

Christ (I)

(see **God**) a favourite subject for blasphemy, much in demand by movie makers and the mass media who variously claim that he was homosexual and/or was married to Mary Magdalene. (see also **Mohammad**)

Christ (2)

A morally undemanding totem figure of **Happy Clappy** Christians

Happy Clappy

Aisle-dancers. Marriage bureau. People who claim to have been born again, whereas they were only born yesterday.

Alpha Course

A church sponsored activity for people with omega brainpower. Pizza and chardonnay clubs

Allah

The compassionate and merciful. The Supreme Being. See **God**. His name must ever be hallowed and never satirised or taken in vain by anyone – least of all the mass media

Mohammad

The prophet of **Allah** to whom be all due honour and

reverence. Myriad lies have been spread about him: that he was a drunkard, a liar, a warlord and a paedophile. These obscene allegations must be repudiated completely. But see **Christ**

Lent

Obsolete A fast. Sometime Christian observance. A cosmetic. A six weeks period in Spring when **consumers** take advantage of the redundant Christian symbolism to go on a **diet** and lose a few pounds.

Ramadan

A fast. The most holy Fast of the Muslim year

Diet

A fast. The only religious observance still honoured in modern society

Consumer

The modern word for **soul.**

Soulmate

Tabloidese for *drinking partner.* Rare use of the anachronism *soul*

Soul music

An emotional depressant

Lifestyle choice

Any pattern of behaviour whatever. *Formerly* a perversion.

Mortal sin

Formerly a wickedness. Now only a **Lifestyle choice**

Like

Spurious. A syntactical solecism. A word that must precede any descriptive or autobiographical account: "It's *like* there is a God innit?" or "It's *like* I was on my bike". Extremely "It was *like like*..."

So that it never happens again

Here's to the next time. See also **ban**

Ban

Any politically-correct prohibition on e.g foxhunting, smoking, English beef etc. Also a token gesture as a reaction to an outrage such as the ban on handguns after children were shot at a school in Scotland. See **tragedy**.

Atrocity

Archaic. Rape, murder, terrorist attack. See **tragedy**

Global warming (1)

A religion. But see **Dogma**

Global warming (2)

A spot of nice weather for a change

Celebrity

Someone you've never heard of

Tabloid newspaper

A newspaper for people who don't want to read the news. See **learning difficulties**

Health

A religion. An obsession. See also **Newspaper** and **Lifestyle**

Domestic Goddess
Television cook with big tits

Mobile phone (1)
A means of self-advertisement. A fashion statement. A public nuisance. *vulgar* a nuisance. Gadget for repeating totemic phrases e.g. *I'm on a train.* Also useful for blowing up the train.

Mobile phone (2)
The most inhumane weapon since the anti-personnel mine

Mobile phone (3)
A gadget for communicating inconsequentiality between dead souls

Mobile phone (4)
Actually there is no such thing as a mobile phone: there are only portable phones

So
redundant e.g. *Tomatoes are SO afternoony.* See also **Like**. Occasionally together e.g *It's like I was so pissed etc*

Wristbands
Formerly identification bracelets. *Currently* advertisements for e.g. prostate cancer, AIDS etc. See also **Feelings, Sentimental Society**

Diversity (1)
Sameness. See also **Multicultural**

Diversity (2)
The range of sexual practices formerly described as perverse

Multiculturalism
Left wing politicians' policy of promoting ghettos

Apartheid
Multiculturalism in, formerly. South Africa – much disapproved by British multiculturalists

Actively
Universal adverb of redundancy as in *I am ACTIVELY seeking* etc

Phone-in
A radio/TV broadcast conversation in which people with **learning difficulties** exhaust the concept of repetition. E.g. *Hi, It's Roger.... Hi, Roger...Hi...Hi, it's me Roger...Hi* etc

Live and let live
The liberal and fair-minded attitude towards eccentric behaviour. See **tolerance** and **homosexuality**. But see also **foxhunting, smoking** etc

Homosexuality
A **lifestyle choice.** But see also **perversion**

Perversion
obsolete an abnormal, disgusting practice. *Currently* a **lifestyle choice**

Beautiful, outgoing girl with her whole life before her

Description, usually by parents but see **partner, live-in lover** of any teenager brutally murdered. Contrast e.g. *She was an ugly unpleasant little sod and we're glad to see the back of her.*

Partner

Temporary participant in serial monogamy

Live-in lover

Cohabitee with whom one is **having sex**

Make love

Have sex

Having sex

A commodity. See **consumer society**

Consumer society

Replacement for what was formerly known as the public realm

The People's

Of the mob. See **Consumer society, tabloid newspaper, music(2)**

Poverty, chastity and obedience

Terrible conditions thankfully abolished by welfare and modern enlightenment

Truth

A fiction. **Spin, Opinion**

Opinion
A view, an outlook as in *Everybody's opinion is as valid as anyone else's*

Spin
That which has replaced truth

Foreign Office
The central authority of Arab states in Britain

Israel
A pariah

Pregnancy
A failed abortion

Literacy
Technical expression of educational experts as in *Megan's standard of literacy is very high: it's just that she can't read*

Numeracy
See **Literacy** - *...but she can't count*

Distinguished
Old, despised, undistinguished or oxymoronic. *distinguished journalist*

Progress
A superstition

M.E.
The principal manifestation of *me-ism.* Indolence, lethargy, apathy, self-obsession

Pedestrian
An aimless wanderer. An obstacle in the street. One with no sense of direction. One who requires hazard warning lights especially when using the **Mobile phone**

Fast food
The formative stage of litter

Town centre (I)
archaic town hall, market etc. Currently **Fast food** outlets. Edinburgh wool shops. DVD stores. Travel agents. *Definition* The universal system of urban homogenisation

Town centre (2)
A rubbish tip. Squalid, filthy landscape created by drunks, drug addicts and "clubbers"

Centre
Outskirts. E.g. *the tyre and exhaust centre/battered wives centre is on the ringroad*

Now
At this moment in time

Yes
Absolutely

Dogs
Essential requirements for use of escalators, as in *dogs must be carried on the escalator*

Cinema, multiplex etc
Places where **Oiks** eat **Fast food**. Movies in which the soundtrack is both deafening and indecipherable

Oiks

The general public. People. *especially* **Young People, Youths.** See also **Trainers, baseball cap**

Trainers

Essential part of the uniform of the **Oik.** Expensive fashion item for **The poor.**

Baseball cap

A mark of intelligence when worn the right way round. See **Trainers**

The poor (1)

People on benefits. Owners of **Mobile phones.** Subscribers to Sky Television. See also **Trainers, Baseball cap, Fast food, Oiks, Football** etc

The poor (2)

The real poor: i.e those not on benefits, who work for a living and whose taxes pay others' benefits.

Eating disorder

Greed. Gluttony. Sometimes accompanied by regular acts of wilful vomiting. See **Slimming, Surgery, Medicalisation of morals**

Slimming

An obsession of fat people. Also **Slimmers**: people on perpetual diets who stay fat.

Diet(s)

A religion(s). Huge source of income for food producers and suppliers

Counsellor

A fraud. Someone who has been on a **Training course** to learn jargon who then fixes a plaque to his wall which licenses him to extract fees for talking useless drivel. See **Psychobabble**

Psychobabble

The language of a **Counsellor.** See also **Sentimental society, Me-ism**

Me-ism

The **Consumer** in his psychological aspect

Their

Politically correct replacement singular noun for *his* or *her*

Narcissistic personality disorder

Psychobabble for **Me-ism**. One suffering from *npd* – a totally self-obsessed twat. As in *The judge said that the teenager who murdered his parents with an axe was not a sadistic and totally self-obsessed twat: he was suffering from npd.* See **Eating disorder**.

Life imprisonment

A short spell in jail. What murderers judged to be "suffering from" **narcissistic personality disorder** receive

Shrine

archaic a small religious building e.g. Shrine of Our Lady etc. Currently a bunch of flowers left where someone has been murdered/killed in a car crash in order that the person providing it can see his name on the gift tag on the television news. See **Sentimental society**

Friend (I)

A person with whom one is acquainted for longer than a **One night stand**

Friend (2)

The associate of a **celebrity** who sells details of the celeb's private life to the tabloids

One night stand

A relationship. See **Meaningful**

Meaningful

Meaningless

Blame

That which must never be attached to the guilty. But see **We are all to blame**

We are all to blame

Corporate neurosis in which people are coerced into blaming themselves when they are in fact blameless. As in *The Muslim fanatic murdered eighty people in the subway…we are all to blame*. Also *we are all to blame for the Crusades, the world wars, the slave trade* etc. Italian ice cream sellers must apologise for the fall of the Roman Empire. See **Political correctness, schools**

Political correctness

Totalitarianism-lite. The moral and political code of the **Liberal establishment.** Satanic. The very Devil, Father of Lies etc.

ASBO

Antisocial behaviour order. An honour. A coveted appellation. See **Oiks**

Texting

Obsessive-compulsive activity

Self-esteem

Narcissism

Self-respect

Uprightness, moral virtue etc. Now replaced by **Self-esteem**

Chewing gum

That which forms a carpet in the naves of great cathedrals and other significant public buildings

Heritage. Heritage industry etc

Promotional material. Commercial exploitation of national historical assets about which **consumers** are largely uninformed. See also **Sentimental society**

Tourist

Foreign **Oik.** Well-heeled British **Oik.** See **Heritage**

Knighthood

Honour given to financial and media supporters of the government, former pop-stars, drug addicts etc

Hate crimes

Crimes against illegal immigrants. See also **Meaningless** as in *Hate crimes you say guv? What's a love crime, then?*

Meaningless

Generally accepted as irrefutably true

Think

Now replaced by *feel*. See **Feelings**

Fantastic

Averagely enjoyable. Routine.

Fill out

Fill in. But see **Diet**

Health and Safety Regulations

A hindrance by which people who might benefit from access to an amenity are prevented by senseless injunctions too expensive to be obeyed. See **Political correctness**

Partially-sighted

Blind. e.g. *as partially-sighted as a bat*

Hearing-impaired

Deaf. e.g. *as hearing-impaired as a post*

Disabled

Fraudulently in receipt of state benefits

Icon (I)

Formerly a depiction of a religious subject regarded as actually possessing the numinous spiritual character of the subject. Currently blasphemous: a **Celebrity** e.g. *pop idol.*

Icon (2)
The lewd Internet image you have to click if you want to subscribe to e.g. *Nasty Sex.* See **Iconic**

Iconic
Fashionably banal. A cliché used to describe the tawdry heroes of the pop music racket. *E.g* Elvis Presley Bob Dylan, Jimi Hendrix. Iconic status is vastly increased when the icon is dead.

Logo
A sacred text of the **Consumer society**

Inclusivity
Equal access for **Oiks**. The abolition of all rational evaluative criteria for admission. See **University**

Dumbed down
The whole of modern society

Contemporary culture
An oxymoron

Soar
Normal increase

Junk food
The national diet. Food.

Nanny state
Example of hypocrisy: i.e. loud government disapproval

of those aspects of public behaviour from which it derives its principal tax revenues: **alcohol**, **junk food** etc

Alcohol (I)

Term used for *a drink* when it is desired to show disapproval: e.g. *young people and alcohol; alcohol abuse* etc

Alcohol (2)

An intoxicating drink taken by Christians when they wish to rejoice and atheists when they are depressed.

Racist murder

The worst way to be slaughtered. Prefer *racially-integrated murder, unprejudiced murder, equal opportunities murder etc*

Banana

Fruit used to demonstrate to junior school children how to put on a condom. See **Sex education**

Dining-table

Obsolete Around which families used to sit for a **meal**

Meal

The ingestation of food while walking in the street, watching television etc

Carrier bag

Device for rustling during concerts and recitals

Social anthropologists

Tourists who stand at the back of church watching the worshippers

Cheers
Portmanteau word: hello;goodbye;thank you; please;excuse me;sorry! look out! It's about time I got some service in this place *etc. Also* Good health! *When drinking* rare

Classic
Any pop song more than five years old.

I
A grammatical fiction

Prestigious
Fashionable, plush

Change
The universal obsession

Leading
Of any practitioner asked to speak about his art, skill, occupation on television: *leading writer; leading fund-manager* etc

Freud
A common misspelling of the word *fraud*

Pressurised
solecism influenced. See **Pressure**

Pressure
As in *is coming under increasing pressure. i.e.* We used to hear arguments instead

Research
Propaganda for which funding is sought

Crescendo
A gradual increase in volume. Not a climax of volume, as the ignorant mass media say, as in *rise to a crescendo*

Responsibility
Irresponsibility. As in *claimed responsibility* for murdering women and children etc

Rights
Demands

Why would you?
Why should you?

Miss out on
Miss

In the park
eg *Proms in the park...three tenors....test cricket in the park* etc. **Touchy feely** get togethers promoted by the mass media. See **Sentimental society**

Loses out
Loses

Crusade
Formerly a series of military expeditions by Christian knights to recover the Holy Places from the Muslims. *Currently* Any obsessive project that catches the attention of the media eg *Susan Lydon's crusading essay "The Politics of Orgasm".*

Drive change
What is always asked for in advertisements for jobs in the public sector. *Must be able to drive change etc*

Mitigate against
Ubiquitous solecism for *militate* against

Apostle
Formerly one of Our Lord's twelve disciples. *Currently* another example of the use of sacred language for profane, obsessive projects. eg *"Germaine Greer was an apostle of sexual liberation"* See **Crusade**

Pacifist
Someone who expects you to die for his principles

No problem
Yes. e.g. *May I have a glass of fizzy water please?*
Answer: *No problem*
But why might there have been a problem?

Of
e.g. *bored of*. Journalists' form of *bored with*

Drawring
BBC announcers' speak for *drawing.* Also *withdrawral* etc

History
Formerly the recorded experience of humankind presented in a chronological order to demonstrate the sequence of events, cause and effect etc to students. Currently as taught in **schools***: Hitler, the slave trade, the evils of imperialism,* **global warming***, the wicked foreign policy of the USA etc*

Schools

Formerly places where the young were introduced to worthwhile knowledge. *Currently* repositories of **political correctness** where the agenda of the **liberal establishment** is disseminated. See **history, literature, literacy, numeracy** etc

Literature

That which is perused by the semi-literate. Stories of sex and violence, sex and **shopping**, sex and drinking/drugging, sex and your star sign. See **world literature, airport novel** etc

World literature

Novels featuring sex, drugs, **shopping** etc in foreign countries

Airport novel

Any novel. Available in all bookshops, supermarkets etc

Victim (1)

An **underprivileged** thug or an **oik** who has committed a (usually violent) crime. See also **Mugger, Hoodie**

Victim (2)

Any member of a terrorist's family. See **blame, we are all to blame**

Victim (3)

One prosecuted by the police for defending himself against his violent attacker

Vulnerable

A description applied to all except the very rich. *We are all vulnerable.* See **we are all to blame**

Vulnerable to eating disorders
Greedy, self-obsessed

Family
Of a group or society. e.g. *We're all one big family here.* Of a football team, any group of workers, **happy clappy church** etc. See **sentimental society**

Happy-clappy church
A middle-class knocking shop/marriage bureau with inferior songs. See **born again, charismatic church** etc.

Born again
Born yesterday

Charismatic church
From the Greek *charism – a gift.* Thus churches for gifted people with pop music, dancing, overhead projectors, preachers using glove puppets etc. See **happy-clappy, born again, sentimental society** etc

Super
Adjective of universal application. Used indiscriminately of everything from a market, a drug/food/holiday/tin of furniture polish etc. Also of branded foodstuffs, *very big.* See **, Superhero, Junk food**

Big
Enormous. See **junk food**

Medium
Very large. See **junk food**

Small

Of food portions, medium-sized. See **junk food**

Momentum

Frenzied emotional activity. Occasional solecism – *the electricians' withdrawal of their labour will add momentum to the stoppage*

Traumatic

Of any mild physical misadventure or disappointment as when one's favourite football team loses a match, a (usually female) long-distance runner fails to win her race, **Andy Murray** gets knocked out of the Wimbledon tennis championships

Islamophobia

Unreasonable dislike of suicide bombers

Beyond comprehension

Routine. Everyday. Of any commonplace horrendous crime. See **So that it never happens again**

Extremist (1)

A person who actually believes what he says he believes

Extremist (2)

Media euphemism for a Muslim. See **Political correctness**

Caring
Mawkish adjective of ingratiation, advertising etc. *Your caring bank/travel agent/superstore* etc. i,e, organisations and institutions which do not care.

Big Brother
A lewd, voyeuristic television show which confirms Orwell's dark social prophecy in "1984" by bathos

Bear with me
Receptionists' jargon for *I am now going to leave you dangling on the end of this telephone listening to Vivaldi for ten minutes.*

Vivaldi
Music for sewing-machine.

Left wing
Political decency. Morality in politics etc. The official politics of the BBC

Right wing
Primitive, fascist, demagoguery. The political persuasion responsible for all the evils of the world, the world wars etc. See **nationalism**

Nationalism
The root of all evil. See **right wing, internationalism**

Internationalism
The moral and decent form of global politics featuring such benign regimes as Stalin's communism and Islam

Hope
Wishful thinking

Focus

Look at. Usually in job advertisements i.e. *will be expected to focus on delivering choice while working autonomously and promoting equal opportunities*

Focus group

The determinant of government policy

Unilateral disarmament

A nation's voluntary surrender of its nuclear weapons according to the argument that to possess nuclear weapons makes a country more likely to suffer a nuclear attack. A false argument: the only country ever to suffer a nuclear attack was Japan, which did not possess any nuclear weapons

Panic

A counter-productive emotional condition which renders the sufferer unable to act purposefully, rationally or constructively. But see BBC news and interview programmes: *The Minister of Health said there is no need to panic YET.*

Self-help book

Best-selling bundle of irrational advice and superstitious maxims which earns a fortune for its writer. See **lifestyle choice**

Industry

Formerly the pursuit of a trade or productive occupation such as farming, fishing etc. The manufacture of durable goods: motor cars, refrigerators, household furniture etc. *Currently* that which does not involve work, a nuisance, i.e. *the music industry, the television industry, the showbiz industry* etc

Centred around
Solecism, journalistic for *centred upon*

Proven track record
A lie on a job application, **CV**

CV
A brief fictionalised autobiography

Implement
Formerly a tool. Currently what one is asked to do in an **industry** e.g. *implement an ongoing process of self-assessment* etc

Deliver
Bring about, introduce, be responsible for. especially **deliver change**

Deliver change
A requirement of all modern **industry.** To create a sense of perpetual confusion so to render all employees insecure and in fear of theirjobs in the management's hope that this will make them work even harder than before.

Exciting
Dull, run-of-the-mill, the same as before. e.g. *exciting new pop single/movie star/TV soap.* Also (at work) *exciting prospects.* Stultifyingly tedious.

Solutions
Formerly of that which is dissolved in water. Currently redundant promotional word attached to the name of any saleable commodity or service. e.g. *furniture solutions; dinner party s~ ; orgasm s~* etc

Proactive
(at work) Frenetically alert, hyperactive, irritatingly interfering. i.e. a condition of keeping your job. See **deliver change**

Communicate effectively
Communicate

Ownership of your role
Be able to work without the boss looking over your shoulder all the time

Awesome
Of anything that produces a spurious sense of excitement. Anyone who can actually do what is expected of him. e.g. *Pietersen's batting is awesome.* cf *Pietersen can bat*

Teensy
usually *teensy bit.* Journalists' baby talk for *little*

Cynicism
Criticism. especially of any aspect of the **sentimental society**

Innovative
See **change, proactive**

Walk the walk, talk the talk
A phrase frequently repeated by those with **learning difficulties.** See also **Management speak**

Management speak
An impenetrable jargon spoken by people who can't manage

Bond
Formerly what a gentleman's word was, a handshake. Currently the **touchy feely** pseudo-homosexual cuddle among football/cricket teams before each session of play

Touchy feely
A deceit. The universal belief that insincere and artificial feelings should be displayed in public at all times. See **sentimental society**

Sustainability facilitator
One who deals with sustainability issues.

Professional
Formerly one who is paid for his work. Currently a self-appointed **expert**

Expert (1)
A person who returns to explain why he got it wrong the first time

Expert (2)
A **professional** who disagrees with other experts

Social worker
Antisocial worker. i.e. any one of a great and diverse army of government employees appointed to destroy the family. See **birth control, sex education, educationist**

Educationist

A failed teacher. An example of the class **professional**

Literally

Solecism: I was literally over the moon, dead in the water, laughing my head off etc

Taboo (1)

Formerly something not mentioned. See **holy**. Currently any obscene practice talked about relentlessly in the mass media

Taboo (2)

Formerly the strictest prohibitions that must be observed at all costs for the preservation of society. Currently a foolish and outmoded restriction to be universally abolished. See **incest**

Incest

A **lifestyle choice**

Holy (1)

Formerly The sacred. What should be respected. But see **awesome**

Holy (2)

A sneer e.g. against a churchgoer, against anyone who takes religion seriously. NB while **Holy (1)** is no longer used to describe Christians, it is reserved for members of other faiths *especially* **Islam**

Islam

The **Holy (1)** faith founded by the Prophet Mahomet. A most venerable tradition

Christianity
An outmoded superstition

Pressurised
Solecism to have demands made upon one

Radical cleric (1)
A Christian priest with fashionably bizarre notions of the faith. A priest who thinks the Creed is bunk

Radical cleric (2)
A Muslim cleric who encourages suicide bombers

Major
The only word journalists possess to designate anything important

Unveil
The only word journalists possess for *announce, launch, propose, describe, outline.* This leads to absurd expressions e.g. *The Minister of Transport unveiled a new stretch of motorway*

As if
Obsolete See **like**

Time-frame
Modern phrase for when

Active consideration
Consideration. eg *under active consideration* about to be ignored. See **actively**

Mixed metaphor
A combination of figures of speech which do not so

much enliven as confuse. Even Shakespeare could be guilty of this *..take arms against a sea of troubles.* This dictionary awards an annual prize for the champion mixed metaphor. The 2011 prize went to the Home Affairs Editor of *The Guardian* for *...puts flesh on the point outlined* (9/8/05)

Saga

Formerly the national historical epic. Currently media speak for any event that lasts for more than a few days e.g. *the saga of Mrs Hoskins' dispute with Mr Walsh over the garden fence*

Bathos

The denouement of any serious matter into farce e.g. the government's policy on illegal immigrants

Target (I)

Something aimed at with the intention to hit it

Target (2)

Journalism something that is merely *reached*. This can lead to absurdities e.g. when the journalist wants to say that the next set of trade figures are likely to be so bad that they will damage the government's economic strategy he says *trade figures to hit government target.* i.e. they will cause the target to be *missed*

Art (I)

Formerly The tradition of pictorial representation, characterised by its technical excellence, creative power and intuitive insight.

Art (2)

Currently Anything – usually vastly subsidised - that

anyone says is art. e.g. an unmade bed; a urinal; a shit stain on the wall; images of aborted foetuses decorating a picture of the Virgin Mary

Socialist

Well-heeled bourgeois who believes that *equality* is good for other people. A supporter of the state education and health systems who usually sends his own children to private school and takes out insurance for private medical care.

Logical positivism

Illogical negativism

Mother's Day

A secular parody of Mothering Sunday. An annual bonanza for manufacturers of greetings cards, florists etc. See **Father's Day, sentimental society**

Father's Day

Nine months before Mother's Day. An American innovation imported to Britain. An annual bonanza for salesmen of socks, ties, whisky, cigars etc. See **Mother's Day, sentimental society**

Halloween

The eve of the forgotten Christian festival of All Saints. Commercial promotion of the cult of evil among children through pretend **witches,** vampires and crass movies about serial child-killers. See **trick or treat**

Trick or treat

A form of blackmail by children going from door to door on **Halloween** demanding money – or else they will put something nasty through your letterbox

Witches (1)
Proto-feminists. Heroines of the feminist sisterhood

Witches (2)
A commercial exploitation of childish fears through movies, television series etc. exploitative entrepreneurs have recently realised that they can double their money by doing the same for wizards

Remembrance Sunday
Formerly a solemn recollection of the fallen of two World wars. *Currently* an annual opportunity for pacifist clergy to preach appeasement. See also **we are all to blame; so that it never happens again**

Advent (1)
Formerly the penitential season preparing for Christmas. *Currently* the climax of the Christmas **shopping** pandemic

Advent (2)
Bizarre journalistic usage for any arrival or innovation. e.g. *since the advent of self-blow up Muslim sex dolls; Old Trafford welcomes the advent of the striker 'snotty' Smith* etc

Media studies
The means to a qualification that is almost guaranteed to bar the way to a career in journalism

Scientific progress (1)
Bizarre description of the process by which every new scientific theory to gain acceptance is a refutation of the theory previously held to be true. The continuous procession of fashions in materialism.

Scientific progress (2)
A slogan for promoting research funding.

Horoscope
Fatuous superstition printed by quality newspapers for fear that its omission would lead to lost sales to the tabloids

Academic (I)
Adjective irrelevant, impractical, purposeless, tedious, jargonistic, fatuous, circumlocutionary

Academic (2)
One who receives taxpayers' subsidy to make a handsome living out of **Academic (1)**

Academic (3)
One whose mind is so fine it has never been penetrated by a single idea.

Young offender
A teenage thug. Apprentice old lag. See **Young Conservative**

Young Conservatives
Marriage bureau for right wing toffs. Table tennis players. Extinct c. 1998

In care
Of a child whose family doesn't care

Nursing
Patient-focussed service delivery (*Guardian* public sector jobs ads)

Empowerment
The professional (social services) attempt to give responsibility to those incapable of it.

Measureable outcomes
Results

Basis
A word used in the circumlocutionary programme to abolish the simple adverb. e.g. *on a temporary basis* instead of *temporarily; on an ad hoc basis* for *ad hoc.* Ad nauseam

Social inclusion
The politically correct policy of including those who, for their antisocial behaviour, ought to be excluded.

Political correctness gone mad
Political correctness. (It's mad already)

Substance misuse
Drug addiction. (Not to be confused with *transubstantiation, consubstantiation* etc*)*

Vision
Formerly a visual apprehension of the divine. Currently in job advertisements: *You will have a vision of.* i.e. *You will fit in with the ideas of the bureaucracy*

Miracle
Formerly an act of God. Currently anything mildly surprising or out of the ordinary. e.g. *It was a miracle when United came back from being two goals down; If the post arrives on time, it's a miracle. usually* used of such events by people who don't believe in miracles

Came back from the dead

Formerly The resurrection of Our Lord. Currently a phrase used to describe what happened when United recovered from being two goals down

Football

Barbarism.

Fun (1)

Any mindless excess on the part of **oiks** usually involving **alcohol, popular music, clubbing** etc

Fun (2)

Sexual promiscuity

Fun (3)

Adjective e.g. Fun Day *i.e.* no fun at all, except for **Oiks** and **Punters.** Fun Outing: a mindless excursion for the above

Popular music

A noise. An oxymoron

Child care (1)

What middle class professionals arrange for their children so they can continue their careers

Child care (2)

As in *child care home* etc. Taxpayer-funded opportunity for the abuse of children

Green

Naive, stupid, immature. *especially* a scientifically-ignorant environmentalist with totalitarian intent

RSPB

Royal Society for the Protection of Birds. An organisation which (1) prosecutes those who cull avian pests and (2) protects the murderous magpie

Bats

Flying mice that foul barns, church belfries etc. Culling them is now a statutory crime

Damaged

Counselling jargon which allows egocentric neurotics to blame their unhappiness on their early childhood

Counselling

Any system of amateur psychotherapy that provides endless opportunity for egomaniacs to talk about themselves. See **Touchy Feely, Sentimental Society**

Therapist

Overpaid sentimentalist with a plaque on his door

Alternative therapist

Overpaid sentimentalist with runes and crystals supplying treatment for hypochondriacs and the pathologically gullible. See **Therapist**

Badgers

Pests enjoying the protection of sentimentalists. See **Bats, Foxhunting**

Foxhunting

The historic sport of England, now a victim of class envy and socialist spite

To bits

Journalistic cliché for *very much*, always followed by a disclaimer: e.g. *I love " Big Brother" to bits but –*

Chaos (1)

Of traffic, communications. Any departure from the perfectly smooth running expected. The mildest disruption

Chaos (2)

The utter paralysis of the road and rail traffic system in Britain following the slightest dusting of snow.

Drought

Extreme and prolonged water shortage in desert countries. In England (a very wet country) what is proclaimed by the water companies each year to divert public attention from their failure to maintain the water-pipes.

Bwuerk
Broadcast journalists' pronunciation of *book*

Really
Metaphysics That which is. otherwise *very* and pronounced (even sometimes spelt) *reely*

Reely reely
Phrase used obsessively by empty-headed (often female) journalists. See also **really**

Children's television
The means for the premature sexualisation and commercialisation of the lives of children. See **Indoctrination**

Suicide bomber
A murderer, usually Muslim

Thank you for calling
Recorded telephone message which means *I am now going to make you listen to a Bach Brandenburg Concerto for ten minutes* See **Bear with me; Vivaldi**.

Babes
Tabloidese for semi-naked young women with big tits. See **Stunna**

Stunna
A **babe** with exceptionally big tits

Brainwashing (I)
A totalitarian method of inculcating party doctrine to the exclusion of all rational enquiry.

Brainwashing (2)

An accusation made by atheists and secularists against the attempt to teach the historic Christian faith to children in e.g. Sunday School. See **Brainwashed**

Brainwashed

As in *I've been brainwashed.* A complaint. The correct response to this is to say, *But in order to be brainwashed, you would need to have a brain to start with*

Bias

What the BBC believes its producers and presenters do not have

Arts Supplement

The enthusiastic promotion of pop music, alternative comedians and clubbing to be found in a weekend section of a newspaper.

Poverty

The condition of deprivation in which unfortunate people enjoy only the most basic necessities of life: *Sky* television; mobile phones; motor cars; designer trainers; kebabs; lager; junk food etc

Sky One

Television programmes for those who find ITV too intellectually challenging

Needs

Wants. See **Special needs**

Special needs

PC phrase used not to denote a process but a person: i.e. *He's special needs.*

Personality
Froth. See **I**

Television personality
Oxymoron. Anyone who appears on television

Reality television
Popular television programmes featuring **oiks** as they overeat, drink to excess, vomit and fornicate. The one who can persist in these activities for longest is adjudged the winner

A Level
The "gold standard" of the English education system. An examination which is impossible to fail

Grammar
Obsolete Outmoded **elitist** insistence that there is such a thing as correctness in word order, punctuation, spelling etc. frequently erroneously *grammer* - especially *Times Educational Supplement*

Grammar school
A socially-divisive and **elitist** institution based on the ridiculous assumption that some pupils are more academically and intellectually inclined than others. The abolition of grammar schools is an obsession of the Labour Party e.g. *I'm going to destroy every f***ing grammar school in the country* – Anthony Crossland

Guilty
Obsolete culpable - from the time when it used to be believed that the individual was responsible for his actions. *Currently* a **victim** of our unjust social order. But see **feel guilty**

Feel guilty
A mawkish emotion expressed by the speaker as a pretended apology for something trivial he hasn't done – usually as a diversion from an actual and genuine wrong or neglect. Also *psych*: See **We are all to blame**

Inspired by
Used in art criticism for *copied from, plagiarised.*

Rote
Pejorative word used by trendy educationists to derogate the wholesome practice of learning by heart

Taste (1)
That which is lacking in the diet of the general public

Taste (2)
Obsolete the notion of refinement. See **discrimination, elitism, judgemental, value.**

Value
The perverse idea that some things – apart from the material – are worth more than others. See **value judgement**

Value judgement
The criterion by which judgements should never be made. See **discrimination, elitism**

Safe sex
All sex is safe, except that which includes the risk of disease, unwanted pregnancy, emotional difficulties, family break-up, disappointment, fear of failure and disproportionate financial expenditure.

Death of the adverb

A recent occurrence in the development of English. e.g. *on a regular basis* for *regularly.* See also **basis**

Universal panacea

Tautology. Journalists' phrase for *panacea*

Row

Journalists' word referring to any discussion whatever.

Time frame

What's the time frame? Redundant phrase for *When?*

Take care

Meaningless but ubiquitous remark universally spoken by people who will see each other again very soon – probably the same evening. See **Cheers**

Right now

Now

Law and Order

Crime and disorderliness in the streets. The policy heading under which the government publishes the doctored crime figures.

War on Terror

Euphemism for the ineffective measures being taken to prevent suicide bomb attacks from Islamofascists

Freedom of Speech (I)

Everyone has it but no one is allowed to use it. See **Political correctness, Institutional racism**

Freedom of Speech (2)
A myth. It's fine to say
What a blessed and glorious thing it is to slaughter people on the London Underground!

Institutional racism
The crime of which we are all guilty and declared by law to be so whether we know it or not. See **Macpherson Report**

Macpherson Report
The report accepted by the government and drafted into law which defines *a racist incident* as *any incident so reported by the victim or any other person.* The most sublime example of the use of words to mean anything at all – and so to be utterly meaningless. A catch-all for **Political correctness,**

Liberal establishment
The politically correct tyranny ruling the country

Consult
Prevaricate

Duty (l)
Obsolete Now only as part of the phrase *duty free*

Duty (2)
Others' responsibility to provide for my **Rights**

Atheism
Hubris

I was sat
Schoolteachers' and BBC journalists' phrase for *I was sitting*. See **I was stood**

I was stood
Schoolteachers' and BBC journalists' phrase for *I was standing.* See **I was sat**

Higher Education
Higher than what? See **A level**

Euthanasia
The principle by which high-minded people arrange the disposal of those who are a nuisance because old and ill

In terminal decline
Rotten. Defunct. The state of town and city centres, education, the NHS, public life in general.

His
Obsolete See **Their**

Different from
Obsolete Now *different to* or *different than*

Studio debate
A slanging match

Invited audience, an
As opposed to an audience of those just barging in

Punters
BBC-speak for *the public.* See **Out there**

Out there
Anywhere not within the confines of Broadcasting House.

Glastonbury
An ancient Christian holy site. Now (1) an annual excrescence. See **Popular music** (2) An agglomeration of shops selling crystals, runes, charms, horoscopes etc. See **New Age**

New Age
Old superstition

Body, mind and spirit
A section of worthlessly cluttered shelves in bookshops, which might otherwise have held books. See **New Age**

Vegetarian
Person who believes it is your moral responsibility to provide him with e.g. a nut roast when he comes to dinner, but will not give you a steak when you go to his place

Peace march
Vacuous gesture. See **Unilateral disarmament, Useful idiots, Popular music, substance misuse**

Useful idiots
Phrase used by the old Soviet Union for unilateral disarmers

Liberal churchman
An absurd person who worships God who, he thinks, might not exist

Lovely, bubbly
Of a young woman *especially* one savagely raped and brutally murdered: *She was a lovely, bubbly etc*

Difference
Euphemism Shockingness, repulsiveness, ugliness.

Birth mother
Mother. *Usually* one late discovered by a sentimentalist as a smack in the face for the adoptive mother who has faithfully brought him up

Cyclist
Pavement hazard for pedestrians

School-run
Twice daily trip in the 4x4 by overprotective, paranoid parents to transport their children the half mile to and from school. Results in clogging the roads, fattening the children and forcing the local **Paedophile** to reschedule his predatory routine

Paedophile
Modern form taken by the bogeyman

Shopping
A displacement activity. An addiction

Social actors
Sociologists' term for *people*

Long term decline
Planned destruction, as of UK fishing industry

Good Friday Agreement
Milestone publicity stunt in the government's surrender to the IRA

Information complex
Archbishop of Canterbury's definition of the soul (newspaper article 20/8/05)

Wool my
London HQ spokesman over the telephone introducing the Royal Mail: *This is the wool my*

Vibrant
Noisy

Moral issue
Unimportant – i.e. not a financial issue

Gifted
Given

Grieving process
That which the bereaved are commanded to endure by psychologists and counsellors

Ban
The statutory means by which the government encourages a particular activity: e.g. the ban on handguns has greatly increased gun crime; the ban on certain drugs has increased the rampant trade in illegal drugs etc

Begs the question
Petitio principi. A loaded question which assumes a particular answer, e.g. *When did you stop beating your*

wife? More commonly, ignorant journalistic phrase for *asks the question*

TV appeal
Our first sight of the murderer. Usually a member of the family of the victim asking for information about the relation he has just raped and slaughtered. See **Lovely, bubbly. Closure. Grieving process.**

Conservative Party
A defunct organisation which existed to promote national sovereignty, free enterprise and low taxation. Now just another version of statism and collectivism

Socialism
A corporatist and collectivist programme for the management of the country. Currently promoted by the **Conservative Party**

Socialist
One who extorts your taxes so he can waste the money on fanciful ideological projects

Edgy
Formerly nervous, on edge. Currently avant garde, the latest thing, as reported in the "music" pages of a **quality newspaper**: *The F***ing Decibels are the edgiest band in town*

Quality newspaper
Formerly a national broadsheet printing serious news, opinion and review articles. *Currently* a national broadsheet – typically turned tabloid – copying the worst trivia of the tabloids in the pursuit of higher circulation. See **Dumbed down**

Outing
Formerly a day at the seaside, in the country, at the opera etc. Currently asserting that a public figure is a practising homosexual e.g. *Peter Tatchell attempted to out the Archbishop of York*

African American
Black

Committed
Devoted to, dedicated. Also used of lunatics and evangelical Christians

Mecca
Centre for anything such as DIY materials, garden furniture etc. Sometimes hilariously e.g. *The Western Isles are a mecca for Scotch whisky* (Sunday Times)

Is
Broadcast journalists' golly-gosh word for *will. The Prime Minister is announcing* i.e. *This afternoon the Prime Minister will announce*

Oral sex
Filthy talk

Disinterested
Ubiquitously used for *uninterested*

Totally destroyed
Destroyed

Hugely
Very

Run down council estate
Council estate

Political correctness gone mad
Political correctness

Progressive
Decadent, degenerate

Progressives
Irrationalists who believe that yesterday was just as bad as the day before, but yet believe tomorrow will be better than today

Reproductive rights
Abortion See **Choice, Woman has the right to do as she wishes with her own body, A**

Choice
Abortion. See **Woman has the right to do as she wishes with her own body, A; Reproductive rights**

Woman has the right to do as she wishes with her own body, A
Abortion. See **Choice, Reproductive rights**

Affirmative action
Politically correct racism and sexism. Discrimination in favour of approved minorities, women, blacks

Jingoistic
Patriotic, conservative, traditional and so abhorrent.

Niggard
Banned word owing to its similarity to you-know-what.

Miniscule
Minuscule

Enormity
Sheer awfulness. But journalists think it just means very big

Primarily
First

Wristband
A fashion accessory to advertise a spurious concern e.g. *make poverty history wristband.*

Man I want to have kids with, The
Formerly Husband. *Currently* Not just one of the guys I'm having sex with. Someone **Special**

Special
Adjective so overused as to be meaningless e.g. *a special programme; a special supplement* etc. Where everything is special, nothing is special.

Baby mother
The woman – one of the women – whom I have successfully impregnated

Power couple
Usually of **Celebrities.** A man-woman shack up in which both are in trendy, highly paid work.

Water-cooler chat
Executives, City workers having prised themselves away from their computer screens to stand in the

corridor talking about last night's episode of **Big Brother**

Retail therapy
Shopping

How... is that?
Formerly an appeal to the cricket umpire. Currently a faux interrogative to express a banal indicative e.g. *How stupid is that? How sexy is that?* etc

In depth
Trivial, showy, long-winded. Of a television documentary, newspaper feature etc. Long. See **Dumbed down; Analysis**

Analysis
In the mass media, longish feature or documentary setting forth the editor's prejudices. See **Studio debate**

Animal rights
Cant. Actually meaningless. Only rational creatures may be said to have rights and responsibilities. See **Duty**

Animal rights activists
Terrorists – to whom the government turns a blind eye - who persecute humans in the name of animal welfare. See **Sentimental society**

Commence
Pretentious word for *start, begin.* Once the sole users of the expression were Methodist ministers: *The Women's Bright Hour will commence* etc. Now the preferred word for *start* among journalists

Life
The mandatory sentence for murder. Currently around three and a half years

News, The
Especially television. Entertainment

Specially
Spurious. e.g. *specially designed, chosen* etc. *designed, chosen*

That
Verbal tic. e.g. *It was like the police were so everywhere and that*

Lord Prescott, Lord Hattersley, Lord Kinnock
Irony

Stress (1)
Accent applied to the wrong syllable by broadcasters

Stress (2)
Formerly the natural result of making an effort. Currently an imaginary property such as phlogiston. A shibboleth. That which must be reduced.

Meltdown
Demise. Lush expression beloved of journalists e.g. *Iraq on brink of meltdown*

Explosion
Increase. E.g. *explosion in elephant numbers*

Of (I)
One of the words which broadcasters choose to emphasise: *We shall have news* **of** the UN summit. Similarly with *from* and *to.*

Of (2)
Currently used in place of *have* in e.g *I must of*

Grooming
Formerly one's turnout, personal presentation. Currently seduction, *especially* of a child by a **Paedophile**

Rocket
Increase. See **Soar**

Shish titty
The noise that leaks from your neighbour's earphones on your train journey. i.e. *shich-titty-shish-titty-shish*

Superhero.
Obsolete a hero from the armed forces. *Usually* a footballer, e.g *Shaun Fouler was Chelsea's superhero in Saturday's battle with Manchester United*

Me
Now universally used by media types to demonstrate their street cred in place of the nominative *I* e.g *me and the series producer was heading for the wine bar*

Cross (I)
Obsolete The instrument used in the Crucifixion of Our Lord, the supreme emblem of the Christian religion. Currently an item of furniture banned from schools, crematoria and other public places for its capacity to offend Muslims

Cross (2)

Christian emblem now not allowed on graves by order of the Diocese of York as to do so would "constitute undue replication of the supreme Christian symbol"

Teddy bear

Formerly a childish comfort. Currently a childish comfort used to ornament roadside **Shrines**. See **Sentimental society**

Novel

Formerly a fictionalised narrative written to illustrate times and manners. *Currently* an illiterate commercial production without intellectual, aesthetic or moral content.

Gender reassignment

Official permission to get the NHS to pay for you to look like a member of the other sex for a while. My be reversed also at the taxpayer's expense

Grief tourism

The new sport of visiting and videoing sites of particularly nasty murders. See **Lovely bubbly, Shrine, Teddy bear**

Medical education course

A process of re-education to which GPs are subjected when they have the gall to suggest to obese people that they just might be a little on the chubby side.

It's

Its

Secret
Something everybody knows e.g. *the government's secret plans to distribute anti-flu tablets to Cabinet Ministers*

Social inclusion
A diktat ordering preference to be given to **Oiks** so spoiling many a pleasant social activity

Morph
Change

Impact
Hysterical word for *affect* e.g. *The rise in imports will impact the trade balance*

Bottleneck
But the frequent expression *will reduce the bottleneck* means the bottleneck will be made even narrower

Mugger
See **Victim (1)**

Hoodie
A violent thief (see **Mugger**) who wears a hood so that he will not be recognisable on CCTV cameras. See also **Oik, Underprivileged, Victim**.

Tate Modern
A disused power station currently used to house rubbish

Positive discrimination
Racism against white people.

Flaunt
Used by journalists when they mean *flout*

Basically
Meaningless verbal tick. *Basically, it's a matter of economics* i.e. *it's a matter of economics*

Equal opportunity
A grammatical fiction by which people are deliberately misled into believing candidates will not be chosen for their ability, suitability etc

Incapacity benefit
A national bribe by which the government aims to guarantee its electoral support from the **underclass**

Underclass
Society's **Oiks.** See also **Poor, Underprivileged**

Poetry
The species of writing which anyone however unintelligent or untrained can produce at will. Any lines of words which don't quite reach the margins

Prayers
Lists of demands to God. See **Rights**

Teetotaller
A person who can stay awake in the late night TV film

Offensive
Normal, decent activities that transgress the code of **Political correctness.** e.g. The Mothers' Union voted to cease praying for mothers and children because such prayers are likely to prove *offensive* to childless women

Satire
The ancient art of ridicule by parody. Now impossible. Anything the satirist can invent in the morning has been surpassed by fresh idiocies in the real world by lunchtime

Home
Especially: in a home. Particularly a child or an old person taken from his home and incarcerated in an unhomely institution.

Civilian
Formerly used of the great majority of people who are not members of the armed forces. Now used to refer to people who are not policemen. But a policeman *is* a civilian.

Apologise
What the British are obliged to do for their history, the church for the **crusades** etc

Trafalgar
Famous British naval victory of 1805 which the government declared must not be celebrated as such for fear of being **offensive** to the French. The battle was re-enacted by a *blue team* and a *red team* instead.

Abnormality, An
An interesting diversity

Cripple
An **offensive** word. Prefer *differently-abled.* e.g. *The Church of St Giles Differently-abledgate*

Alcoholic (1)
Anyone who drinks more than his doctor

Alcoholic (2)
Former drinker who gets together with other former drinkers to talk endlessly about how much they used to drink

Electric guitar
Instrument of torture

Moog synthesiser
Musical instrument for non-musicians

Administration
Delay.

Administration Block
An office building for e.g. the NHS or the education service created to maximise delay

Archbishop
Post-modern ecclesiastical figure who believes that theological doctrines may be applied only ironically and in inverted commas e.g. *'I "believe" in "God".'* – Rowan Williams

Church of England
Secular left-wing pressure group

Christening
Opportunity for universal use of digital cameras. Prelude to the booze up and the cake

Wedding
Fashion parade. Excuse for a piss up. See **Christening**

Bigamy
Double error

Conversation
Simultaneous soliloquies

Dentist
Professional person who fills his pockets by extracting your money

Doctor (1)
Medical professional subjected to insulting behaviour and vicious abuse by **Oiks**

Doctor (2)
Go-between the patient and the undertaker

Drama
Any mundane event milked for mass sensationalism by the media

Eating
Loathsome street activity by **Oiks** prior to dropping litter

Freemasonry
Gentlemen's club persecuted by the General Synod of the Church of England

Feisty
Adjective of an hysterically aggressive, vulgar woman

Sunlit uplands
Optimistic prediction, which usually turns out to be fog-shrouded peaks

Hell
Seventy-two Muslim virgins

Hangman
Formerly revered public servant now made redundant by **Progressives**

Scoutmaster, Clergyman etc
Synonym for **paedophile**

Bible
Discredited collection of ancient myths and fables believed only by **Fundamentalists.** But see also **Koran**

Fundamentalist (l)
An unreconstructed primitive irrationalist. An idiot. But see **Muslim**

Fundamentalist (2)
Someone who actually believes what he says he believes

Muslim
A worshipper of Allah, the one true God and a disciple of the Prophet Mahomet

Koran
A most venerable and holy book of spiritual truth. But see **Bible**

Lawyer
Professional class of official receiver of other people's money

Accountant
Chartered extortioner

Liar
Politician

Love rat
Celeb who cheats sexually one celeb with another celeb

Love child
Accidental bastard

Journalists
Infallible collection of professionals entirely above reproach, expert at finding fault with every institution in the world.

Gun crime
Shootings and murders in Britain, which have increased threefold since the government banned handguns

Body count
Journalists' aphrodisiac

Communism
The second most cruel and inefficient despotism in history

Intellectual
Common misspelling of *ineffectual*

Academic
Handsomely-subsidised obfuscator of the blindingly obvious. Person paid to translate what everybody knows into words no one can understand

Advertising (1)
A corrupt commercial practice by which people are encouraged to buy what they don't want with money they haven't got

Advertising (2)
The whole essence, form, style and character of everything that is said on the mass media.

Appearance
That which, in order of significance, has now replaced reality

Lwuerk
Broadcast journalists' pronunciation of *look.* See **Bwuerk**

Sassy
A western African tree *(Erythrophleum suaveolens)* of the pea family, having bark that yields a poison and wood that is used for construction. Word used by obsessional fashionistas for *chic*

Positive
Originally *definite.* Now *optimistic.* Promotional word – see **Upbeat**

Upbeat

An unaccented beat or beats that occur before the first beat of a measure. Also called *anacrusis.* Commonly used to mean mindlessly sanguine

Rap (I)

A blow to the head – usually by a **Musician** spouting racial and social prejudices in tedious rhythm and failed rhyme, urging violence towards women

Rap correspondent

Music critic on *The Guardian* who approves of rap

Musician

Adulated noise-monger

Chasm

Journalists' word for any gap, however small. See **Gap**

Gap

Always prefixed by *yawning*

State of the art

The latest gimmicky version of a product or technique. Also *cutting edge*

Football

A religion of sponsored barbarism for **Oiks** involving public displays of cursing, spitting, endemic violence and hefty bribes

Neutral umpire

Umpire

Value added tax
Payment for thin air. A fraud

Extra virgin
Obsolete What does she do for the *extra* bit?

Appraisal
Management technique used annually to frighten and coerce employees. See also **OFSTED**

OFSTED
Government method of terrifying and handicapping schoolteachers and ruining children's schooling by rigid bureaucratisation

Initial stages
Ponderous phrase for *at first.* See **Commence**

Best practice
Labyrinthine procedure designed to hinder the job in hand

Focus group
Rigged committee of members of the public that provides the government with an excuse to claim that the policies it will impose are democratic

Capital Punishment
The just punishment for murder, since the abolition of which murders in Britain have increased twelve-fold. See **Democracy**

Bach flowers
Remedies for sale to trendy, gullible women. See **Alternative therapist**

Body, mind and spirit

Section in bookshops of paperbacks providing superstitious treatments. See **Psychology, Counselling, Spirituality.**

Psychology

Derived from the Greek word for *soul.* Fraudulent practice by quacks and charlatans who don't believe there is such a thing as the soul

Spirituality

Formerly the condition of the soul in a life of prayer and devotion. *Currently* any faddish attempt to gain spurious emotional satisfaction.

Big bang

Modern creation myth. The prevailing superstition among cosmologists

Slimmer

A fat person who pays good money to be told lies about how to get thinner without eating less

Obesity

The usual condition of the habitual dieter

Condom

A panacea. *usually* in the injunction *Wear a condom* – the nearest sex education gets to morality.

Empower

Politically-motivated policy to give power to those who would only use power catastrophically. See **Oiks, Underclass**

Minorities
Politically-preferred sub-groups of undesirables

Brutal murder
Journalists' phrase for *murder.* See also e.g. **Vital clue, Gap** etc

Vital clue
Clue. See **Brutal murder** also *vital role, acutely aware* etc

Crisis
Any series of events in which the outcome is in even the slightest doubt. *e.g. crisis talks, government crisis, crisis at Old Trafford etc*

Antiracism
The policy of preferring black people before whites

Free!
A commercial promotion. See **Free gift**

Free gift
Tautology. See **Free**

New
Worse

Major player
Slang important influence, institution, agency etc

Burgalry
BBC reporters' word for *burglary*

Mixed ability

Part of the comprehensive system of education which prevents intelligent, well-behaved children from learning by putting them in classes with stupid unruly louts

Abnormal

Obsolete unnatural, perverse *especially* in sexual behaviour. *Currently* interesting **diversity**

Abuse

That which child-molesters and rapists claim they suffered as children in order to excuse their crimes

Accident

An opportunity to sue – *usually* a public utility – for damages

Proactive

Interfering

Sin

*Obsolete*a crime against God. Currently a lifestyle choice

Adultery

What all adults are expected to commit

Alcopop

A variety of highly sweetened alcoholic drink produced to encourage children to take up drinking as a lifetime habit. Pretend cigarettes used to perform the same function for the tobacco industry until **political correctness** banned them

Bring to life
Kills, ruins, makes a travesty of. *e.g The production of the opera which dresses the protagonist in leathers and sets the action in a New York skyscraper apartment really brings "Don Giovanni" to life.*

Morbid
The style of pop songs

Attitude
Random belligerence adopted as part of **lifestyle.** See **Feisty**

Architect
Destroyer of buildings, spoiler of cities, apostle of ugliness and inconvenience in public spaces.

Boring
Anything requiring an attention-span of longer than five seconds

Brilliant
Brash, tawdry, mindlessly exciting, frequently obscene *e.g. The band swore at the audience and threw up on the stage – it was brilliant*

Bulimic
Posh Latin word used euphemistically as a clinical description for the gluttonous young women who habitually make themselves vomit because their vanity will not allow them to risk getting fat

Burglar
Nocturnal thief who enjoys the protection of the law against householders who defend their property against his incursion

Cathedral
Formerly a holy place, the metropolitan church of a diocese. *Currently* a tourist attraction

Party, partying
Formerly a gathering of friends over dinner or of children to play musical chairs and eat jelly. *Currently* chiefly used in its verbal form *infinitive, to party – to drink excessively, take illicit drugs and fornicate indiscriminately usually against a background of* **Pop music**

Censorship
Effectively abolished concerning the stage and cinema, including blasphemous slurs on the Christian faith. Retained only to prevent criticism of **Islam**

Ceremony
Unceremonious usurpation of a formerly religious occasion. Glossy, trashy event *e.g. Oscars' Ceremony, Britpop Awards Ceremony etc*

Compliance
A system of rules and prohibitions in the workplace and other public institutions designed to hinder industry and retard progress

Controversial
Sexually explicit, exhibitionist, trite, blasphemous, run of the mill – i.e. *uncontroversial*

Cookery Programme
Television entertainment for people who eat only packaged supermarket food

Decision-making process, the
Deciding

Deference
Outmoded politeness, an offence against **inclusivity**

Diana
Horsewoman. Lady who hunts. Woman bent on remaining single. Goddess of hunting and chastity

Dianafication
The sentimentalisation of society, vastly accelerated since the death of the Princess. See **Lovely bubbly, Shrine** etc.

Planet, the
The earth. Our home. *The planet* makes it sound as if the speaker is talking about somewhere else and alien.

Save the planet
An anti-capitalist slogan

Literary editor (1)
One who knows everything about the last two or three pulp-fictional best-sellers and nothing about literature

Literary editor (2)
Spoiler of authors' manuscripts

Embryo
Human tissue used for research purposes.

Epic
Long

Era, age, epoch etc
A brief period of time *usually* referring to passing fashion e.g. *era of punk rock, Spurs supremacy etc*

Public library
Noisy video, DVD store where reading is discouraged.

Fluke
A good shot by your opponent

Fat (1)
Officially disapproved food item

Fat (2)
Adjective people who diet

Time-bomb
Spurious media hype for any unfortunate outcome that was entirely predictable. *e.g. obesity time-bomb, AIDS time-bomb etc.* An especially appetising recent example *diarrhoea time bomb*

Media hype
The television news

Responsible
That which someone else is for your misfortunes

Crime
Socially-conditioned behaviour from which the poor are unable to abstain. This definition is objected to by the millions of poor people who are not criminals.

No blame culture
The demoralised society, Britain today. Culture in which all blame for wicked, criminal and antisocial acts attaches to someone other than the perpetrator

Fault
That which attaches to someone else

Impact on
Affect

Role
What everybody has. e.g. *Plays the role of the bishop/headteacher/chairman* – so giving the impression that no one actually does or is anything in reality but only *plays the role of*

Address (I)
Ask – as in *address the question.*

Address (2)
Face – as in *address the issue*

Fun-loving
Description, appealing for help to catch the killer, at a televised press conference of his daughter by the tearful father who has just murdered her. See **lovely bubbly** etc

Education
Inferior modern replacement for teaching

Anguish
Disproportionate disappointment e.g. *Kidman anguish at Oscars snub* or *Missed penalty anguish for Beckham*

Die with dignity
To be complicit – *especially* an old person – in one's murder at the hands of the doctors

Hyperactive
Usually of a child: undisciplined, delinquent, hysterically out of control. An example of the **medicalisation of morals**. See **surgery**

Surgery
An MP's availability in his constituency. It implies that his constituents are sick

Medicalisation of morals
The redefinition of a character defect in terms of disease. See **Eating disorder, hyperactive, drinking problem** etc

Drinking problem
Dipsomania, gluttony for alcohol

Attention deficit disorder
Refusal to pay attention. Sheer indiscipline in children. See **medicalisation of morals**

Post-traumatic stress disorder
Formerly shell shock

Special clinic
Burgeoning non-judgemental treatment centres for the indigenous VD

Non-disabled
Approved word for the politically-incorrect *healthy, whole* etc

Chronic fatigue syndrome
Morbid indolence, torpor, usually resulting in narcissistic and hypochondriac withdrawal from social intercourse

Personality disorder
Character defect, moral flaw.

Burn survivor
Approved phrase for *disfigured person*

Recovering alcoholic
Non-drinking so-called alcoholic who meets with likeminded people to talk endlessly about how much they used to drink

Substance dependence
Drug addiction

Developing countries
Countries that never show any signs of developing

Freedom fighter
Terrorist aiming to establish a totalitarian tyranny

Activist
Terrorist

Exist
Of being. *People* exist. *Objects* are merely extant

Credit
Debt

Infamous
Notoriously vile, abominable. But now used of any error however trivial e.g. *The Liverpool striker's infamous penalty miss*

Tory
Formerly one who held the constitutional respect for the monarchy and the establishment of the Church of England. *Currently* a politician who seeks office by adopting the policies and style of the Labour Party

Feel
Formerly *think.* See **Feelings, Touchy-feely, Feel guilty**

Filth
See **Adult**

Flout
Used by all journalists to mean **Flaunt**

Folk singing
Barristers, stockbrokers and dentists caterwauling over pints of beer about the loveliness of the lives of miners, Irishmen and the lumpen proletariat

Liberation
Paradoxical word for what communism always promised to deliver from its ideology of determinism and inevitability

Barbecue
Suburban irritation. Gratuitous noise. Pollution

Guitar

Formerly a classical stringed instrument of great beauty on which the music of Bach and Rodriguez was played by virtuosi such as Segovia and John Williams. Currently abused, ill-played and deliberately smashed by exponents of **Popular music**

Hoodie

Formerly a Royston crow. *Currently* a *usually* young person who seeks to hide his identity while committing acts of theft and vandalism

Impetus

Journalists' word, always used absurdly. *e.g. The support of the dockworkers for the miners' strike will add impetus to the stoppage*

Narrative

Gobbledegook. A made up story. Politicians' lies. *e.g. The candidate's narrative is structured out of a more caring, less confrontational agenda*

Butter

A taboo substance by which – so we are informed throughout the mass media – the grocer is trying to murder us with a heart attack.

At risk

To be the victim of one's own perverse whims. *e.g.* (a probation officer on Radio Four) *My job is to identify those at risk of committing a crime.* See **In danger**

In danger

Usually from oneself. *e.g. Those vulnerable people in danger of using drugs, binge-drinking etc*

Halloween

Formerly (Christian) the eve of All Saints Day. *Currently* a pagan-commercial celebration of horror films, occult games for children etc. *crass Today is the eve of Halloween.* See **Trick or treat**

Liver transplant

An operation much dreaded by all human livers in case they found themselves transplanted into George Best

Grieve

What the family of murder victims can do only after they have given an emotional TV press conference. See **Move on, closure**.

Devastated

The landscape after a severe hurricane, earthquake, tsunami etc. Also used to describe the emotional state of one whose team has just lost a football match

Privacy

That aspect of people's lives which is observed only by TV cameras and subsequently discussed endlessly in the papers

Confidence, full confidence

That expressed fervently by the Prime Minister in a member of his cabinet immediately before he sacks him.

Modern educational methods

Systematic prevention of learning

Nucular

BBC presenters' word for *nuclear*

Battle with alcoholism
Being perpetually pissed and having one's occasional fits of phoney remorse choreographed for TV and the tabloids

Hard line, right winger
A person with right of centre views appearing on BBC news programmes

Highly respected, influential
A person with left of centre views appearing on BBC news programmes

Inimitable
Imitated everywhere

Journey
Long emotional wallow e.g. *I'm on a journey to find myself.* To which the answer should be *Well, I wouldn't start there*

Parliament
Former representative legislative body, now a tool of government **spin doctors**

Spin doctor
Government liar. e.g. *If you're accusing me of making up the truth, I plead guilty* – Peter Mandelson 2005

Weather forecast
Prolixity. e.g. *snow event* (for *snow*). *Night-time period* (*night*) etc

Stigma

Formerly a useful warning by public censure against a harmful practice. *Currently* an unjustified slur that must be removed and hang the consequences for the prevention of suffering. e.g. *the stigma of AIDS*

AIDS (1)

A disease spread chiefly by sexual promiscuity

AIDS (2)

A cause celebre. cf **Red Nose Day, Children in Need** etc

Red Nose Day

Media event grandly organised to exploit the **Sentimental Society**

Children in Need

cf **Red Nose Day, Sentimental Society** etc

Suffers from (1)

Complains of

Suffers from (2)

Perpetrates, is the origin of. e.g. *suffers from* **Attention Deficit Disorder, Narcissistic Personality Disorder** etc

Team Building

Companies' practice of taking away their senior staff for the weekend, fill them full of drink and encourage them to shag one another indiscriminately in order to promote a guilty solidarity that the company hopes will translate into deepened corporate loyalty and increased productivity

Bonding

Mawkish psychobabble for what was formerly *bringing up the children*

Kids' Television

The training of children in consumerism and banal lifestyle

The Times, Daily Telegraph etc

Sensational, lurid advertising magazine. *Formerly* a newspaper

Sexual somnambulism

Having sex in your sleep. An acceptable excuse for rape in the British courts

Infectious laugh

Said of any young woman murdered, *especially* a nurse, teacher or police officer: *She had an infectious laugh*. So that at first one wonders whether that was what she died of

Funeral

Formerly obsequies according to the Book of Common Prayer, a Requiem Mass etc. *Currently* a Schmaltzfest with maudlin pop music, teddy bears and an Address which doesn't mention God, death, salvation or the life of the world to come. See **lovely bubbly, infectious laugh**

Like a football

As in *The defendant allegedly kicked the victim's head like a football.* Heads are always kicked *like a football*

Marginalised

Usually applied to members of the shiftless underclass of oiks. Actually, the truly marginalized are those who hold traditional views of any sort – old-fashioned Tories; adherents of the Book of Common Prayer; well-mannered people generally

Deteriate

The word used by BBC reporters and presenters (especially Radio Four) for *deteriorate*

Ecce Homo

Colloquial Lancashire expression for *O look, there's a homosexual!*

Enlarge

Word used in the imperative with reference to the penis. The first word of most emails that arrive in your box overnight.

Enlightenment

An historical period in the 18th century when atheism, noble-savageism, political correctness and state executions were introduced under the guise of liberty, equality and fraternity

Equal

What people are not and never have been

Erection

Formerly a structure, a building. Currently second most common word to arrive in your email box overnight.
See **Enlarge**

Evolution
A theory of the origin of species used by atheists to explain the meaning and purpose of all human activity

Devolution (1)
The policy of a centralising government to give authority in insignificant areas of legislation to ever-smaller provinces

Devolution (2)
The UK government's policy of giving Scottish people a say in the concerns of the English – without reciprocity

Centre of Excellence
A rare educational institution appointed to contrast with the rubbish that goes on everywhere else

Expletive
An adjective in a modern movie

Flesh
Human flesh. A commodity

Folk music
Songs about rustics and peasants sung heartily by left-wing schoolteachers, lawyers and dentists

Alienated, the
People who are subsidised by the taxpayer because their cluelessness and general stupidity makes them unable to find their way around in normal society

Freak show
Many of the shows that appear on Saturday evening television

Genealogy
Ancestor worship for the middle class

Secret, secretly
Something that everyone knows all about as in *America is secretly arming the secular militias against the Islamic regime in Somalia* (newspaper report)

Criminal (1)
One who has his **rights** protected by the **police service**

Criminal (2)
An unfortunate person oppressed by economic forces

Police service
Formerly the police force. *Currently* a taxation-funded organisation for guaranteeing generalised political correctness - e.g. investigating a Muslim leader for his faith's disapproval of homosexual practices (Britain 2005)

Convenience food
Packaged rubbish fit only for throwing down the lavatory

Train (1)
A connected series of moving compartments for the use of mobile phones

Train (2)
Late-arriving mode of transport. The customary environment for **Mobile phones, oiks, Shish titty** etc

Newspaper (1)
The by-product of a collection of advertisements

Newspaper (2)
A moralising instrument which itself is above moral accountability

Newspaper (3)
A record of the doings of **celebrity** with extensive **lifestyle** sections. May contain some casual, uninformed opinion

TV drama
A sentimental or oversexed parody of the police, hospitals, office girls etc

Radio comedy
Oxymoron Unfunny Left wing agit-prop

Football
The Colosseum with bungs

London transport
Still life

Overseas aid
Taxing the poor in rich countries to give to the rich in poor countries

Organic
Poncy stuff twice the price of the normal veg

Sex education
Consists entirely of the slogan *Wear a condom*

Share with
I'd like to share with you. i.e *Stand there and listen while I bore you to death*

"Crimewatch"
A BBC television programme in which pornography is dressed up as public service.
See **terrible murder; Mr**

Terrible murder
To be contrasted with *nice, friendly, gentle murder*

Mr
Courtesy title now not used – except to refer to convicts

Guy
Formerly man. *Currently* anyone: man, woman or child. Coming soon *guyhole-cover; deep third guy; guy-eating tiger* etc

Presentation
What governments now produce instead of policies. See **Spin**

Bereavement counselling
Grief by numbers

Friends of the planet
Enemies of mankind

Decision
A word always prefixed by *tough*

Opportunity
Always prefixed by *real*

Challenge
Always prefixed by *stark*

Challenges
Problems

Lifestyle
Always prefixed by *sustainable*

Existing age profile
Age

Putting a ceiling on
Limiting

Healing process
Sentimental phrase for any act of spurious emotionality. e.g. *The Church of England is to hold a march to commemorate the abolition of slavery. It will begin the healing process*

Massive hunt
Hunt. e.g. a police search. cf *Massive heart attack* .i.e. a heart attack. Examples of hyperbole.

Supermodel
A model. See **Massive hunt** etc

Stand in line
Formerly *Queue.* e.g. *Would you stand in line for 32 hours for the King's College Carol Service?*

Trained marksman
A marksman. Contrast with *untrained marksman*

Negatively impact upon
Damage

Move into a more active phase
Act

Is located at
Is at

Underachieve
Fail

Haitch
aitch

Groom
Corrupt

Is comprised of
Comprises

Down to
Up to

Absolutely clear
Clear

Upcoming
Forthcoming

Very much so
Yes

A whole raft
Plenty

Reduce down
Reduce

Revert back
Revert

Between you and I
Posh ignoramus phrase for *between you and me*

Back to back
One after the other - as in *back to back Test matches*:

Contact phone number
Phone number

School community
School

Detrain
Get off

Basically
A redundant expression. No more than a verbal tic

A big ask
A difficult task

Added bonus
Bonus

Decimate
Formerly Reduce by one tenth *Currently* wholesale destruction

Dedicated car park
Car park

Drive down costs
Reduce

Fallen pregnant
Pregnant

First up
First

For free
Free

I'm good
(No you're not!) I'm well

In actual fact
Actually

Issues
Problems. *He has issues with drink*

Meet with
Meet

Next up
Next

Sexed up (1)
Exaggerated

Sexed up (2)
Excited

On a daily basis
Daily

PIN number
PIN

Pan fried
Fried

Oven baked
Baked

Please RSVP
RSVP

Potential risk
Risk

Regular
Medium (of portions)

There you go
There you are

Run it past you
Mention

Plan ahead
Plan

Quantum leap
An infinitesimally small change – not a great jump

Close proximity
Near

Paramount
Uppermost

Focussed
Concentrated

Gender
Sex

Face time
Make a point of seeing colleagues (business-speak)

Leading author
Media cliché-hype for an author. (See also leading *scientist, philosopher, musician etc*)

Advanced warning
A warning

Bear with me
Wait

Bigging up
Enlarging

Blue sky thinking
Bureaucrats' foolish optimism

Carbon footprint
Alarmist slogan used by those who preach the superstition of **global warming**

Creative writing
Purple passages of nauseating **self-expression**

Self-expression
Egotism – a form of idolatry

Modern
A universal slogan among all politicians and publicists. See **New**

Policies
Advertisements. Gimmicks. Words without deeds

Recycling (1)
Getting on one's bike again

Recycling (2)
Time-wasting, uneconomic way of getting rid of rubbish slowly

Wind turbines
Ugly, useless machines by which environmentalists ruin the environment

Tree
A large plant. But in the City of London a sacred object which the Corporation will on no account allow you to prune, pollard or trim – not even when its fallen leaves block gutters and cause untold damage to an ancient church, Grade One listed building etc

Environmentalist
A variety of terrorist. See **Tree, Global warming, Wind turbines** etc

Climate change
Weather

Alcohol issues
Formerly navy rum ration. *Currently* drink problems

Respect
What feral youths demand immediately prior to shooting/stabbing you

Initiative
Especially **new**. publicity stunt by government which has no initiative

From here on in
In future

Deeply sophisticated
Profoundly shallow

Government
Nationalised advertising

Hospital
A place. Extravagantly sponsored by the taxpayer, where one goes to contract fatal diseases such as C-difficile and MRSA

General Synod
Church institution which meets twice a year to express its denial of traditional Christian teaching

Church of England
The New Labour Party at prayer

Bus service
Something that has been discontinued, abolished or otherwise removed – cf Post Office, doctor's surgery, telephone kiosk

Gun
An object now possessed by violent criminals only, following the government's ban on their legitimate use

Journalist
Cliché-monger. cf **unveil.** Also *hijacked, ramped-up, pressurise, miss out on* etc ad nauseam

London
Everlasting traffic jam

Clubbing
An activity involving (1) baby seals or (2) fornicating, drug-addled pop music fans

Smoking
One of the very few remaining crimes along with parking

Chef's soup of the day
Soup

Live golf
TV programme. An oxymoron

I hear what you say
I'm not deaf

How easy is that?
That's easy

Key report
A report, the conclusions of which are approved of by the speaker

Controversial report
A report, the conclusions of which are not approved of by the speaker

Government policy
An advertisement

English Premier League
National football competition where the teams are all made up foreigners

Peace campaigner
Hindrance, bloody nuisance, idiot

Pacifist
One who believes it is wrong to use force to defend a child from enemy violence

Disability allowance
Government bribe

Public sector workers
New Labour's client state

Pension
Something received by **public sector workers** paid for out of the government-raided pensions of private sector workers

Florist
A member of the class of the new super-rich thanks to the proliferation of **roadside shrines.** See also **touchy feely, lovely bubbly**

Drug addict
Pop music celebrity given knighthood for services towards the corruption of youth

Weapon
An item of sports equipment as in the police request to competition pistol shooters to *hand in your weapons*

Morning hours
BBC weather forecasters' phrase for *morning*

Frightened of
Frightened by

Personal journey
New Age phrase for narcissism, self-obsession

Inner self
A grammatical fiction

Literary festival
A gathering of hippies, advertisers and other illiterates, often sponsored by the BBC

Any time soon
Soon

Church bell-ringer
Touchy, drunken atheist who turns up to disturb the peace

Official rate of inflation
Government statistic about half the actual rise in the cost of living

Team leader
Boss

Incentivise
Encourage

Let's touch base about that offline
Can we have a private chat?

Capture your colleagues
Make sure the other bastards turn up to today's pointless meeting

Paradigm shifts
Changes

Cascade
Tell everybody

Cascade down
But did you ever see a waterfall going upwards?

In negative territory
Of the Stock Market: ie *down*

Talking the talk and walking the walk
Merely doing the appropriate thing

Holistic approach
A fudge

Respected sociologist
A sociologist

A Male
Eg (police-speak) A male was seen running away. A man

Burglary gone wrong
(police-speak) A burglar violently assaults/kills a householder. This is described as a *burglary gone wrong* implying that the burglary was going well until that moment

Murals on walls
Murals

Forward planning
Planning

Head to head
Competing

Battling with alcoholism
Lying on the sofa consuming cans of strong lager

Bretwalda Books Ltd